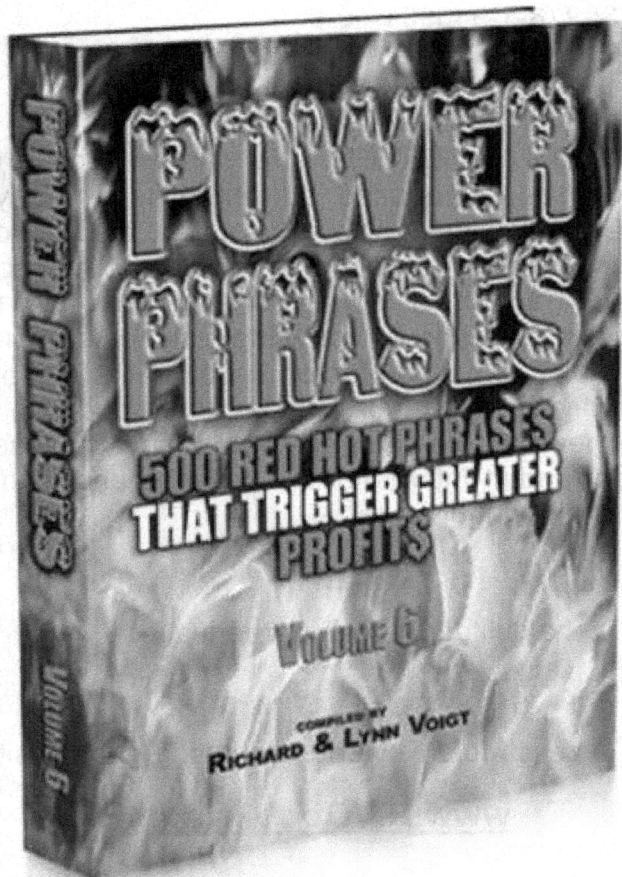

POWER PHRASES – Vol. 6
500 Power Phrases That Trigger Greater Profits

To Access More Powerful Marketing Tools Visit:

www.RIVObooks.com

www.RIVOinc.com

www.WisconsinGarden.com

POWER PHRASES

Volume 6

500 POWER PHRASES THAT TRIGGER GREATER PROFITS

-·|·-•·*""''*·•·_·-|·-•**•-·|·-•·*''''''*·•-·|·-

Compiled by

Richard & Lynn Voigt
I.M. Education Specialists

Introduction:

Powerful Phrases, Headlines, Sub Headlines, Slogans, Bullet Points and Interview Sound Bites are perhaps the most powerful marketing tools mankind has ever created. They are the lifeblood behind every business venture are the ultimate secret weapon of Millionaire Marketers.

No matter whether you are introducing or promoting a brand new product, teaching a "How To" skill, building a website, or simply sending an email, using the perfect power phrase is crucial to capturing and holding eyeballs and producing greater marketing profits.

In today's world every word you use has measurable impact. Each word can produce emotional psychological buttons that trigger psychological reactions. Successful advertisers understand that using an effective power phrase is a true art form that turns "wants" into instant gratification "needs." Once artfully triggered, any niche market can instantly create more protifable conversions.

Now it's your turn to personalize this incredible collection of 500 Power Phrases in ways that instantly advance your own effective marketing skills as you create new and power phrases, slogans, presentations, bullet points, or interview sound bites that take you to the next level.

Whether starting or running a small business, writing an ad, coming up with a memorable slogan, making a major corporate presentation, bullet points, creating a video, writing a book, searching for the perfect slogan, teaching a lesson or book report, your creative use of these Power Phrases can capture more eyeballs and produce some amazing rewards quickly turning you into a Marketing Genius. Now, it's your turn to make the magic happen!

POWER PHRASES

Volume 6 – 2501 - 3000

500 Power Phrases That Trigger Greater Profits

Begin Selecting & Customizing Your Perfect Marketing Phrase

2501	Earn Money With Your Computer
2502	The Compelling Essence Of Making Money
2503	Is Success About Manipulating People
2504	Casual Smart And Modern
2505	Shock Till They Drop
2506	Everybody Sings The Blues Sometime
2507	Essential To Human Reasoning
2508	Ugly Ad Will Out Pull A Pretty Ad
2509	The Shock Doctrine
2510	Finding Lost Customers
2511	Peripheral Players In Marketing
2512	Grateful You Bought My Book And Actually Read It
2513	These Are All High Quality Downloads
2514	Benefit From A Robust Online Economy
2515	Rewriting History
2516	Keep Your Brand Natural
2517	The Important Keys To Success
2518	Find Great Deals Everyday
2519	Article Directory
2520	Less Than Half Price
2521	Who's Buying This

2522	Old Digital Trash
2523	We See I To Eye
2524	The Digital Revolution Is Already Here
2525	Benefit Layden Bullets Are What Sell The Product
2526	A New Millionaire Is Created Every Hour Are You Next
2527	Quickest Way To Achieved
2528	Create A Powerful Free Gift
2529	How To Stop Your Divorce
2530	Here's A Run Down Of What's Included
2531	The Size Of Audience Doesn't Matter
2532	Are You Really Ready To Become An Entrepreneur
2533	Here's My Objective
2534	Eliminate Fears Holding You Back
2535	The True Role Of Entrepreneurs
2536	Features Tell But Benefits Sell
2537	Make Sure Customers Have A Fair Choice
2538	Need A Helping Hand With Your New Business
2539	I'll Give You The Keys To My Malibu Mansion
2540	How's Your About Page
2541	All In A Single Stroke
2542	If You Create It
2543	See How Crazy It Gets
2544	How To Make Salesletters Interactive
2545	Why Keep Going Down Blind Marketing Alleys
2546	Stop Messing Around With Losers
2547	There Are Words That Will Keep You Poor
2548	Here Are Some Of The Great Things You'll Enjoy
2549	We Want To Hear The Story
2550	This Will Change Your Life Forever
2551	Look For Pain Plus Urgency
2552	Accomplish More In Less Time
2553	Choose A Niche Within A Niche
2554	Why Social Media Isn't A Career
2555	Zero Results Never Again
2556	Making Money Guide To Real Wealth
2557	Flexible Perks
2558	The Key Is - Not On Their Own
2559	This Is Something You Should Not Miss

2560	It Sounds Like A Smart Move
2561	Want Massive Traffic
2562	Hidden Impact
2563	Those Shiny Object Just Drain Money
2564	Solid Home Business
2565	Every Internet Marketer Needs This System
2566	Rant And Rave
2567	What Are You Going To Be
2568	You'll Want To Catch This
2569	Speak Your Message
2570	Trial Offers Are Extremely Scalable
2571	Celebrity Is The New Currency
2572	Really Big Mistake
2573	Point Your Browser To…
2574	Includes Video For Higher Conversions
2575	Foolish To Close This Door
2576	Minimum And Maximum Price Ranges
2577	It's Time To Break The Impasse
2578	No Cancellation Fees
2579	Start With Nothing And Publish
2580	Two Tools I Always Use
2581	A Well Oiled Money-Making Machine
2582	Appropriate Pricing Strategy
2583	From Drab To Fab
2584	Did You Fall For This
2585	Your Dreams Realized
2586	What Now
2587	Create Cliffhanger To Seal The Deal
2588	Avoiding The Humiliation Of Rejection
2589	Building Ultra Responsive Lists
2590	Invest In Your Brain
2591	Your Read It Correctly You Keep All The Commissions
2592	Are Your Values Expanding Your Potential
2593	I'm Not Charging A Penny For This
2594	Tap Into Their Wonder
2595	Add Fun To Life
2596	These Transactions Can Dramatically Benefit You
2597	Find A Market With A High Ticket Product

8

2598	Who Uses Mail Anymore
2599	What's Your Unique Benefit
2600	Pulling Buyers In From All Directions
2601	We Have Work To Do
2602	Losing A Great Deal Or Getting It
2603	Why They End Up Pulped
2604	There's A Problem
2605	Let Me Join Your Team
2606	Long Form Sales Copy That Makes Money
2607	Reducing Your Power
2608	I Quit Using Adwords Forever
2609	Learn This Trick For Yourself
2610	The Best Framework Ever Discovered To Teach Others
2611	You Learn A Lot About Your Business With This Conversation
2612	Get Adventures Out Of A Smile
2613	Clickbank Calculator Software
2614	This Is Where High I.Q. People Fail
2615	Time To Upgrade Your Life
2616	Access The World Of Source
2617	Death Of Yellow Pages
2618	You Can Cancel Whenever You Want
2619	Flair And Classy Clothes
2620	Most Powerful Opt-In System Ever Created
2621	Ideas That Die Well
2622	Popularity Focused
2623	This Becomes Exceptionally Helpful
2624	Start Research Curious Background Stories
2625	Never Turn Back
2626	Your Million Dollar Rolodex
2627	Sit Back And Watch The Money Flood In
2628	I Agree One Hundred Percent
2629	Building Block Solutions
2630	It's Not Always About Working Hard
2631	Sell Your People First
2632	Everything You Really Need To Know
2633	Register Early
2634	You'll Never Ever Have To Pay For Advertising Again
2635	A Great Headline Can Be Worth Millions

9

2636	Your First Cash Register
2637	Don't Just Become A Spare Part
2638	Warning This Information Will Change Your Thoughts
2639	Right Now Is The Crucial Moment To Decide
2640	Have You Ever Had Someone Like This In Your Life
2641	How To Zip
2642	No More Struggling
2643	Audio Books
2644	Leverage Their Mentality
2645	New Hope For Struggling Marketers
2646	Guaranteed To Fill Over And Over
2647	Can You Handle Having Power Over Others
2648	Do You Need A Revolutionary Idea To Bring To Market
2649	How To Achieve Reality
2650	Personal Strategies, Habits And Secret Tools
2651	Adwords Scheduling
2652	Create An Amazon Two Pizza Team
2653	Multiply Your Profits
2654	Notice Some Honest Marketers
2655	When Do You Need It
2656	Order Now, Pay Later
2657	Spreading Cell To Cell
2658	Hire Professional To Do That
2659	You're Invited On My Next Cruise
2660	Going Off The Grid
2661	Succeed As A Consultant
2662	No More Just Looking Responses
2663	Willing To Really Start Today
2664	We Grow Money Not Hair
2665	Escaping The impending Rat Race
2666	You Won't Pay $997
2667	Laughing Too Little
2668	Doesn't Have To Be Difficult
2669	Conflict Resolved
2670	Why Most Experts Only Have A Job
2671	Sustain Your Voice Longer
2672	Start Using These Headlines In Your Business Now
2673	How About A Double Dose Of Secret Shattering Tips

2674	Here's The Basic Idea
2675	Convert Visitors Into Subscribers!
2676	Doesn't It All Seem Undaunting
2677	I Did It The Unselfish Way
2678	Perhaps I'm Getting Ahead Of Myself
2679	Instant Solutions To Frequently Asked Questions
2680	Impact Of Random Events
2681	Black Friday II
2682	Police Your Own Money
2683	A Name For Your Product
2684	Move It Into The Cloud
2685	Hit Different Triggers
2686	Satisfy Curiosity
2687	It's Just Too Easy
2688	Will The Internet Replace Your TV
2689	Snockered And Unstable
2690	Tricks And Techniques For Skyrocketing Profits
2691	Visual One Page Project
2692	Bad Boy Busted
2693	Enormous Swings
2694	Experimentation Is Key To Innovation
2695	Create Bigger Paychecks Fast
2696	Your New Partner Does Want You To Succeed
2697	That's Also The Upside
2698	How To Make Money Even When You Fell Rotten
2699	Marketing Pain Shouldn't Get In Your Way
2700	Tools Designed For Me
2701	Did You Really Miss This
2702	Imagine The Potential Sales
2703	Shortcut Secrets
2704	Life Without Limits
2705	The Central Figure
2706	Partly Conscious Approach
2707	The More Focused The More Success
2708	The Average Hospital Bill Has $600 In Phony Charges.
2709	Your Personal Stimulus Plan
2710	Something Big Is On The Way
2711	The Tweeter Generation

2750	Create A Lasting Brand For Yourself Online
2751	Free Traffic
2752	Just How Powerful Is This
2753	What To Do With Your Subscribers
2754	Master Information
2755	Simple Research That Brings You Wealth
2756	The Most Profitable For You
2757	Online Meetings Made Easy
2758	Lot Of Tools And Resources
2759	In The Spiral Of Things Getting Worse
2760	Does Your Mic Rustle When You Talk
2761	Just When You Thought All The Good Ideas Were Taken
2762	Ever Wanted To Buy It All
2763	They're Not Laughing After I Made My First Dollar
2764	Sales Letters Are Not Dead
2765	Writing The Rules
2766	Alleviate Stress In All Your Customers
2767	Manage Any Size Network
2768	Get This Rebrandable eBook Now
2769	Analyze Your List Carefully For Flaws
2770	Marketing Eyeball Assault
2771	10 Eye Popping, Jaw Dropping Ad Copy Secrets
2772	Video Search Engine Optimization
2773	Legal Espionage
2774	Are The Rumors True
2775	Startling News Flash
2776	The Only Stupid Question Is The One Never Asked
2777	The Best Short Cut You'll Ever Find
2778	Why They Just Tune Out
2779	Web Tool Development
2780	Release Your Limitations
2781	Now Is The Time To Learn
2782	I Know You're So Rich You Don't Need This
2783	Don't Know About PLR
2784	Set It Up And Walk Away
2785	Free Crystal Ball That Tells All
2786	Spillover Profits
2787	Use Buttons And Links To Test Your Order Now Links

2788	Why Some Businesses Survive And Thrive In Hard Times
2789	Why Should I Take A Closer Look
2790	Right Help At The Right Time
2791	Her Crazy Sense Of Humor
2792	Green Is The New Gold
2793	Embed These Into Your Headlines
2794	Why Did They Say NO
2795	Need Some Time For Yourself
2796	How To Only Invest Time Not Money
2797	All You Really Need Is One Simple Idea
2798	Super Goal Setting Secrets
2799	Simplest Steps People Use To Succeed
2800	Pick Up A Free Sample
2801	The Power Behind Expectation
2802	The First Thing You Need To Know
2803	Step Into Nature
2804	Why Must You Win
2805	No Roadblocks Or Barriers To Enter
2806	They All Skim Around Your Offer
2807	Last Minute Bonus
2808	I'll Walk You Through This Exercise
2809	Yeah I Really Do It Myself
2810	Start Out With Quality
2811	Make Money Playing Online Poker
2812	There's No Hook
2813	Hang On Because It Just Gets Better And Better
2814	What If I Offered You Something Unique
2815	It Shows Me Where To Go
2816	What's The Catch - There Is None
2817	Quit Challenging Everything And Just Do It
2818	Move The World With A Longer Leverage
2819	Power Of The Past
2820	Now You Too Can Kiss Your Internet Worries Goodbye Forever
2821	Join Our Winning Team
2822	I'm Not Going To Oversell This
2823	Do Just The Opposite And You'll Succeed
2824	Combining The Right Mindset
2825	Break It Down - Making It Simple

14

2826	There's No Faster Way To Grow
2827	Maybe You'll See What I Saw
2828	Clickbank Vendor Cloaking Secrets
2829	White Label Products
2830	Don't Wait For Something To Happen
2831	Avoid Wanting A Bigger Vision For Yourself
2832	Let's Fix The Problem
2833	This School Is In The Clouds
2834	Double Down
2835	I Became An Internet Marketing Sponge
2836	It's A Must
2837	Stop Refunders And File Sharers
2838	Your Humanity Makes You Relatable
2839	Entertainment At A Great Price
2840	Select High Profile Partners
2841	The Greatest Online Navigator Will Steer You Toward New Horizons
2842	Prove Your Worth
2843	Compile A 100 Day Ecourse
2844	How Prepared Are You
2845	Tantamount Terror
2846	Oh Yah Money Money Money
2847	Stealing Your Money
2848	Bargain Basement Bonanza
2849	No Previous Experience Required
2850	Send The Traffic To You First
2851	Look At What You Get For Free
2852	Clarity Supported By Action
2853	Don't Know Where To Start
2854	How Can We Add Another Product To Our Menu
2855	Extraordinary Residual Income
2856	Is The Life Of A Child Worth $1 To You
2857	Sense Of Urgency
2858	Don't Be Transparent Be Authentic Instead
2859	Gaining Global Clout
2860	No Swiping Allowed
2861	Because I Know My Stuff Is Good
2862	Don't Allow Your Inner Critic To Censor Your Ideas
2863	Full Details In Seconds

2864	Access Opportunities When Listening To Customers
2865	Who Do I Know That Can Solve Your Problem
2866	Chalk One Up
2867	Stages Of Buyer Awareness
2868	Our Goals Are Pretty Simple
2869	Recipe For Disaster
2870	Does Your Business Still Struggle With A Negative Bank Account
2871	When Shipping And Handling Pays For All Of It
2872	Inspire And Engage Your Sales Team
2873	Host Your Site Online Within A Collaborative Environment
2874	Hypnosis Vs. Computer Games
2875	Can You Keep A Secret
2876	Free Comprehensive Survey Allows You To...
2877	Want To Work With Like-Minded Marketers
2878	Think I'm On To Something BIG
2879	Start A Profitable Membership Site
2880	Traffic Success Solution
2881	How Much Pain Do You Require
2882	Would This Totally Change Everything
2883	Limited By DeFacto Standard Marketing Practices
2884	All The Matters Is What Your Customers Need
2885	When Your Image Isn't Working
2886	Cashing Out After Cashing In
2887	How To Protect Your Online Business
2888	Focus On Developing These Tips Not Tricks To Become Success-ful
2889	Sloppy Thinking Equals Loss
2890	Refine Your Marketing Sonar
2891	Works Beyond Expectations
2892	Home Business Opportunities
2893	Pad Your Wallet
2894	A Product that Pays Residual Income
2895	See And Touch Your Target
2896	Confidence Worth Observing
2897	Freedom From Daily Problems
2898	You Know You Can Become A Teacher
2899	Everybody's Got Their Niche
2900	Online Training Is Exploding
2901	Throwing It Together Quickly Produces Junk

16

2902	Build Income Not Just A Business
2903	Start Early And Live Long
2904	Pull The Trigger Now
2905	Buying Businesses Simplified
2906	Start Banking Your Profits
2907	Promote Monthly During The Last Week
2908	Seeking A Serious Collaborative Effort
2909	How To Handle Life's Frustration
2910	Every Hero Has A Downfall
2911	Looking For That Special Boss
2912	Gardening Is My Graffiti When I Grow My Own Art
2913	Enjoy Life While Doing The Right Thing
2914	Stoking Your Own Fires
2915	Make Your Point Stick
2916	Undisputable Champions
2917	You're Faced With THREE BIG PROBLEMS
2918	How To Win The War Of Internet Marketing
2919	Success Is The Fruit Of Learning
2920	Failure Due To Bad Design
2921	Holy Fakes
2922	Dreamweaver Squeeze Video Settings
2923	Master Customization Rights
2924	Watering Yourself Down
2925	Before I Get Started
2926	Looped And Duped
2927	Pull An All-Nighter
2928	You Need To Know This Information
2929	Making Tough Decisions
2930	Cyber Competition
2931	It's Official
2932	Tuck It Behind Your Ear
2933	Your Download Is Free
2934	So Damn Obvious
2935	Why People End Up With Your Money
2936	Ad Must Get Their Point Across
2937	Fine Tune The Quality Of Your Business Innovations
2938	Avoid Looking Down
2939	Blog Set Up Themes

2940	Want A Business That Makes Money
2941	Earn On The Internet
2942	Nothing's Going To Stop You Now
2943	What Do You Need In Order To Achieve That Result
2944	Brand Names Use To Mean Better
2945	Identify Profitable Topics Within Your Niche
2946	Without Buyers A Business Dies
2947	Taking Steps To Close The Gap
2948	Has Your Mail Server Been Blacklisted
2949	Continual Battle To Keep Subscribers
2950	Snatch This Up
2951	I Want To Find Out More About You
2952	What's Expected Of You
2953	Are You Prepared To Be Wrong
2954	Make Contact With Your Audience
2955	Do You Want To Go All Out
2956	You're Getting A 30-Day FREE Membership
2957	Doable For Anyone
2958	How To Extract The Data
2959	What's The Steepest Goal You've Set
2960	Deep Breathing And Meditation
2961	Don't These Drive You Crazy
2962	Speed Up Your Income
2963	Accentuate Your Features
2964	So Why Are You Doing It
2965	Big Decisions Deserve Thorough Due Diligence
2966	Turn On The Fire House Of Submissions
2967	You Can Wish All You Want
2968	Recording The Path To Freedom
2969	Back To School
2970	Let Me Tell You A Story
2971	Growing Faster Than A Wildfire
2972	For Quick Information Call...
2973	How To Choose The Best Program For Max Profits
2974	Based Upon What Best Fits Your Needs
2975	Please Stop The Frustration
2976	Be Just As Proud
2977	Take Immediate Action

2978	Reduce Frictional Unemployment And Save Money
2979	This System Will Never Saturate The Market
2980	Increase Your Search Visibility
2981	Give Yourself An Instant Pay Raise
2982	Stop Being Tossed In The Trash
2983	Become A Business Wizard And Pave Your Way To Success
2984	An Impressive Ear Piece
2985	Start Down Your Own Road
2986	Free Instant eBook Download
2987	Where Are You Right Now Really
2988	Propelled By Rhythm
2989	Look For The HOT Bonus Inside
2990	Amazing Offer Sets Marketing On Fire
2991	Relentless Marketing Will Expose An Urban Myth About Money
2992	Maybe The Truth Is Not What You Want To Hear
2993	Taylor Made For You
2994	Don't Just Hand Out Your Business Cards
2995	Dealing With Abstract Marketing Ideas
2996	Keep Your Headlines Sans Serif Font
2997	Network Like A Pro
2998	Are You One That Makes Things Happen
2999	Wish I Had Written That
3000	Put This In Your Sleigh

Lynn and I hope that this "Think Tank" volume series of 500 Hot Phrases will helped you clearly paint your dreams, sell your ideas, and market your messages, propelling each of your ideas and projects toward incredible success. Watch for our next Volume!

We truly wish you the very best and look forward to hearing your success stories.

Concluding Thoughts:

Ever success is built upon a preparing a strong foundation, having a clear vision, and taking positive action each and every day. If you've been searching for a new lifestyle, then you'll find this book directive and inspirational. You can open it to any page and let that page help you rethink possibilities, consider new ideas, open new opportunities, and ultimately experience a more successful and fulfilling lifestyle.

Every problem has a solution! Regardless of your current situation or circumstance, know that you have the power and responsibility to redirect your life in any direction you choose. Simply start thinking about and research the kind of lifestyle that truly appeals to your heart. Begin your new journey by learning everything you can about your chosen subject. When you make that commitment, you'll open more unexpected doors to unique opportunities than imagined.

"Creative Thought Is The Only Reality
Everything Else Is Merely The By-Product Of That Thought."
- Walter Russell

So why not start thinking **BIGGER? It won't cost you any more.** It all starts by never allowing your current life's situation, environment, or so-called friends to limit your path to a happier, healthier, and successful life. After all, whose life is this?

Make a decision to focus on learning something new each and every day. Begin attracting your ideal lifestyle by doing something you love and enjoy. As difficult as it may be, don't allow money to limit your dreams. Focus on the kind of thoughts that make you feel good. Once you learn how to control your focus, you'll have a great chance to see your dreams take shape. You've finally learn to harness the power you always had within, a Universal Energy stream that flows 365/24/7 in any direction your project your thoughts, Good or Bad. Want proof? The thoughts you currently believe and project reflect the life you're currently living. Therefore, if your life isn't happening, change your thoughts, and change your life. It's something only you can hold, visualize, and project, living your dream come true.

Find yourself a mentor and spend more time with people who truly appreciate, support, and foster your dreams. Life may be short, but the thoughts we hold can make our life wider and more fulfilling.

About The Authors:

Richard and Lynn develop creative strategies that paint dreams, sell ideas, & market messages   Together, they present a unique team-approach, working side-by-side, helping clients pursue their passions while sharing their skills and diverse expertise as authors, artists, inventors, entrepreneurs, & Internet marketing education specialists.

Teaching by example, they mentor proven self-publishing services, graphic design, video production, domain acquisition, and marketing research of behalf of their company, RIVO Inc – RIVO Marketing, since 1997. They've created & produced hundreds of videos, self-published dozens of books on a wide variety of topics and created thousands of original works of fine art, while refining their Internet Marketing techniques, mentoring programs, and related business website development.

Their mission is to continually uncover new products and services, test new strategies, and network useful solutions with off and online entrepreneurs, small business owners, writers, local artists, models, teachers, students, and marketing professionals.

Their goal is to help clients create an action plan that discovers and connects the missing pieces of the success puzzle. The goals they foster create multiple streams of income for today's volatile economic climate. Their motto is: "Do the work once and allow the work to create additional streams of income for a lifetime."

Feel free to contact them if you have questions or would like to tap into their talents and expertise. They appreciate your feedback and look forward to hearing your success stories.

Contact:
Richard & Lynn Voigt - RIVO
I. M. Education Specialists

RIVO INC - RIVO Marketing
13720 West Keefe Avenue
Brookfield, Wisconsin 53005 – USA
Email: support@RIVOinc.com
Website: www.RIVObooks.com
Website: www.WisconsinGarden.com

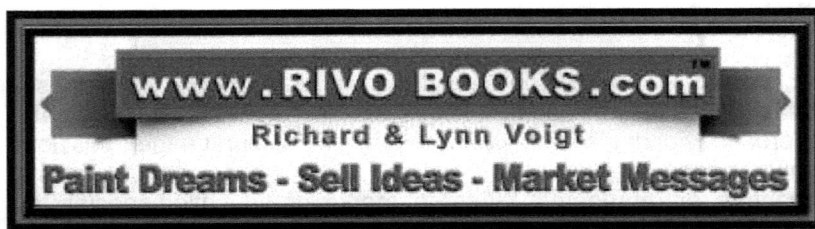

YOUR RIGHT TO WEALTH
Becoming Wealthy Isn't Hard When You Know How

WI GARDEN – Let's Get Dirty
Our Wisconsin Garden Guide Promoting Delicious, Healthier Home-Grown Fresh Food, With Tools, Tips, & Ideas That Inspire Gardeners!

MONETIZE YOUR SOCIAL LIFE
Earn Extra Income While Having Fun Online

BABY NAMES
21,400 Unique Baby Names & Nicknames

FUNNY HEADLINES vol. 1
3,500 Outrageous Silly Brain Toots

FUNNY HEADLINES vol. 2
3,500 Outrageous Silly Brain Toots

JOBS
10,240 Career Paths That Can Change Your Life!

MONEY WORDS
Powerful Phrases That Million Dollar Copywriters Use To Make Piles Of Cash On Demand!

GARDEN QUOTATIONS
400 Garden Quotes From The Earth To Your Soul

HEADLINE STARTERS
175,000 Words That Paint Dreams, Sell Ideas, And Market Your Message

BABY NAMES
25,350 Baby Names & Nicknames For Your Family Friends & Pets
    697 pages 7,000 Names with Origin & Meaning plus Top 100 Names, And 2,000 Most Popular Names

CURIOUS WORDS
15,800 Words That Expand Your Mind And Change Your Life

INSPIRING THOUGHTS
That Inspire Happiness, Success & A Clearer Understanding Of Life

MARKETING EYEBALLS
100 Ideas That Can Add Unlimited Subscribers To Your Lists

SECOND OF FIVE
My Early Years- From Birth To High School

POWER PHRASES – Individual Volumes 1 - 10
500 Power Phrases That Trigger Greater Profits

POWER PHRASES Pro Edition – Volumes 1-10 (Complete Series)
5000 Power Phrases That Trigger Greater Profits

COMING SOON! – BE THE FIRST TO GRAB YOUR PRO COPY

<u>POWER PHRASES Pro Edition</u> Volumes 1-10 (Complete Series)
5000 Power Phrases That Trigger Greater Profits

What do Marketing Millionaires know that you don't? They know how to pull money out of thin air by using their secret language of <u>Power Phrases</u>.

This Pro Edition of <u>5000 Red Hot Power Phrases</u> not only saves you time and money but will help jump-start your creative brain in ways you may have never considered. Simply open this amazing collection to any page and find your perfect power phrase. All it may take is simply adding or replacing ONE word. It's simple, quick, and easy!

1. **Want to create more powerful profitable campaign offers?**
2. **Thinking of revitalizing a more professional business identity?**
3. **Want to update old product or service media advertisements?**
4. **Searching for fresh ideas that could improve sales and profits?**
5. **Looking for brand new ways to create stronger media sales copy?**
6. **Ready to use millionaire strategies advancing you to the next level?**

<u>5000 POWER PHRASES</u> is exclusively for professional Internet Marketers, authors,advertisers, executives, business owners, TV & radio reporters, entrepreneurs, administrators, managers, supervisors, teachers and students who want to find and access unique phrases for marketing slogans, presentation bullet points, and interview sound bites that powerfully paint dreams, sell ideas, and market your message.

Stop wasting valuable time, money, and energy racking your brain for new ideas. Create more profitable power phrase marketing campaigns for all your products, services, slogans, bullet points, and interview sound bites that finally grab and hold people's attention and trigger greater profits?

You now have a very powerful and professional marketing tool in your hand. We are confident that you know how to use it wisely in order to maximize the potential of all your marketing campaigns! Lynn and I **Thank You** for your support and purchase.

CLAIM 500 MORE POWER PHRASES!

Thank you for purchasing this eBook and in doing so we would like to send you **500 More Red Hot Power Phrases for FREE!**

When you post a **positive review of this Book on Amazon Books** under this title you'll receive an additional **500 POWER PHRASES.** Your review may also be sent directly to us.

Your request must be received within 30-days of purchase. Once your positive Book review is posted and verified, simply email the following to **(500@RIVOinc.com)**:

1. Full Name of Purchaser
2. Email address
3. Paypal Invoice Number
4. Copy of your posted Book Review*

Once we receive the above, we'll send you 500 Power Phrases **(PDF)** emailed to the address you provided.

Visit: www.RIVObooks.com for additional volumes as they become available including the Pro Edition of 5000 Red Hot Power Phrases that say what you mean to say and trigger greater profits.

Lynn and I look forward to your written comments and suggestions as we love hearing from each of our readers.

Richard & Lynn Voigt
RIVO Inc – RIVO Marketing
13720 West Keefe Avenue
Brookfield, Wisconsin 53005 USA
Telephone: (262) 783-5335
www.RIVObooks.com

P. S. If you love gardening, catch us on www.WisconsinGarden.com

*NOTE: This offer is valid providing it does not violate the terms of service of the entity with whom you made this purchase. Duplicate or incomplete entries will also not be eligible and this offer is limited to one request per email address. All eligible review submissions become the property of RIVO Inc - RIVO Marketing – RIVO books and may be used as promotional testimonials ads on RIVO Inc websites. This offer may be withdrawn at any time without prior written notice.

www.ingramcontent.com/pod-product-compliance
Lightning Source LLC
Chambersburg PA
CBHW060709280326
41933CB00012B/2365